Contents

Note: When Muslims say the name of one of the Prophets, they say 'Peace Be Upon Him' afterwards. This is shown in Arabic as ﷺ in this book.

Festivals in the Sun

Summer is a wonderful time for festivals. The weather is good and everyone enjoys outdoor celebrations. Since ancient times, people across Europe have honoured the power of the sun at midsummer. Many kinds of fruit, vegetables and other crops ripen in the warm months. Jewish people celebrate this harvest at Shavuot (see pages 8–9).

The weather is hot and sunny in many countries during June, July and August. In India, Hindus hold a spectacular outdoor festival called Ratha Yatra. The festival honours Krishna, whom many Hindus see as the Lord of the Universe. Hindus in other countries hold similar festivals.

A family enjoying a summer picnic with delicious fresh fruit.

The magnificent Ratha Yatra festival in Puri, India. You can see all three chariots.

This book looks at festivals during the summer months in the **northern hemisphere**. Remember that on the other side of the world – in Australia and New Zealand – it is winter then. And in **tropical** countries, such as the Caribbean islands, it can be hot all year round. Also, note that the Muslim festivals are not fixed according to the seasons. The Muslim festivals you read about can take place at any time of the year.

Geeta's Ratha Yatra

'Every year, the Lord of the Universe and his brother and sister go on holiday. The images of the gods travel in amazing chariots, and everyone helps to carry them. I went to the temple dressed in my Indian clothes. We took it in turns to pull the chariot and sang beautiful *bhajans* – our hymns. My cousin in Puri in India says that thousands of people go to the procession there.'
Geeta, Chicago, USA

5

The Martyrdom of Guru Arjan, June

This Sikh festival is a *gurpurb*. *Gurpurbs* are special days to remember the births and deaths of the ten Sikh **Gurus** (teachers).

Guru Arjan, the fifth Guru, spent his life spreading the Sikh faith in India, about four hundred years ago. The Emperor of India accused him of writing bad things about Hindus and Muslims in the Sikh holy book. Guru Arjan said this was not true and refused to change the book.

The Guru was captured and tortured to death. He was pushed into boiling hot water and covered with baking hot sand. The poor Guru was not allowed to drink even a drop of water.

Sikhs handing out free cool drinks in memory of Guru Arjan.

Amar remembers Guru Arjan

'It was actually raining today so we just had to imagine it was hot! At the *gurdwara* (Sikh place of worship), we heard the story of Guru Arjan. We talked about how everyone should be allowed to follow their own religion. Then I helped to give out free drinks. We gave people *kachi lassi* – it's made from milk and water with sugar, and I quite like it.'
Amar, London, UK

An image of Guru Arjan. Many Sikhs have died for their religion.

At this *gurpurb*, Sikhs remember Guru Arjan by giving away free cool drinks to people of all communities. They remember how the Guru stayed calm and cool throughout his terrible torture. It is hot in India at this time of year so people are very pleased to receive a refreshing cold drink. This friendly custom shows that the Sikhs want to get on well with people from different religions.

Shavuot, May or June

Shavuot is a joyful Jewish festival to celebrate the wheat harvest. In Israel, this falls in the summer. Jewish people go out to the fields to sing and dance among decorated sheaves of wheat. Around the world, people decorate their **synagogue** with fresh summer flowers. They bring fruits, just as in ancient times they brought the **first fruits** of the harvest as a gift to the Jewish temple.

Israeli children decorating pretty baskets with flowers and wheat to celebrate Shavuot.

Rachel's Shavuot

'At the synagogue, we listened to a talk about the Ten Commandments. They are rules for how to be good in life. Then it was party time! We'd decorated the place with flowers and everyone had brought their favourite summer fruit – I brought apricots. My favourite Shavuot food is cheese-filled pancakes called *blintzes*. My granny makes them. Her cheesecake is yummy too.'
Rachel, Toronto, Canada

Cheesecake is a popular dairy food at Shavuot.

Shavuot is also the time when Jewish people remember how God gave them the *Torah*, their holy book. It includes the **Ten Commandments**. Some people stay up all night studying the *Torah* and praying.

A spread of delicious dairy foods is prepared for the festival. Various stories explain the reason for the custom. It is said that when the Jews first received the *Torah* laws about how to prepare meat, they didn't quite understand them. So they ate dairy and other foods until they had worked them out. Another story says that the *Torah* is nourishing for the Jewish people just as milk is good food for a baby!

Pentecost, May or June

Pentecost falls at the same time as the Jewish festival of Shavuot. The Bible describes how Jesus' followers met fifty days after he had risen from the dead. Since Jesus' death, they had been scared to go out and tell people all about him. Now, they gathered together and were filled with the Holy Spirit – the power of God.

Helping other people is part of doing God's work in the world today.

Flames and a dove are symbols that represent the Holy Spirit. A dove represents the Holy Spirit's arrival. The first Christians described how it felt like flames on their head. The Holy Spirit gave them the power and the confidence to go out and spread Jesus' message in the world.

This was the beginning of the Christian Church. So Pentecost is the birthday of the Church. Christians celebrate their faith, which helps them to continue God's work in the world today.

This woman has decided to become a Christian and is being baptized.

Lili's Pentecost

'At Pentecost we went to church and watched my friend's baby brother being baptized – he looked so sweet! Afterwards, we went home and had a meal with some friends and lit candles to make it a special occasion. Mum and dad talked about when I was baptized as a baby. It means that I'm part of the Church family. Later, I filled a basin with water and baptized my baby doll.'

Lili, The Hague, The Netherlands

Pentecost is a popular time for welcoming new people into the Church through **baptism**. During a special ceremony water is poured over the person. Most churches baptize babies. Some baptize older children and adults who have decided for themselves to join the Christian community.

11

Poson Day, June

On Poson Day, Sri Lankan Buddhists celebrate the time when Buddhism came to their country. Over two thousand years ago, Emperor Ashoka of India became a Buddhist. He was so enthusiastic about his new religion that he sent Buddhist teachers to other lands.

His son Prince Mahinda travelled to Mihintale in Sri Lanka. He told the King of Sri Lanka about Buddhism. The King became a Buddhist straight away and many men became followers. Women wanted to become Buddhists too. Emperor Ashoka sent his daughter, Princess Sanghamitta, to Sri Lanka and she helped women to join the religion.

The biggest Poson Day celebrations are in Mihintale. The weather is hot so the festival is held outdoors. There is a big procession, with giant floats carrying statues of people from the story of Prince Mahinda. Elephants wearing colourful coats surround the statues, and drummers accompany the procession.

Huge crowds attend the temple in Mihintale on this special day.

12

Hema's Poson Day

'Poson Day is my favourite festival. It gets really busy in Mihintale because thousands of people come to worship here. In the morning my family went to the temple and I joined in the *puja* (our worship). We heard a talk about Prince Mahinda too. Later we joined the procession. It went really slowly through the streets, and the drummers let off fireworks – it was brilliant!'
Hema, Mihintale, Sri Lanka

Around the world, Sri Lankan Buddhists go to their temple on Poson Day. They listen to a talk and make **offerings** to the temple. Festivals are an important time to be generous.

Making an offering of beautiful flowers at a shrine in Sri Lanka.

Midsummer's Day, 21 June

In the **northern hemisphere**, Midsummer's Day on 21 June is the day with the most hours of daylight. Summer celebrations are held all across Europe. In the northern countries, people are delighted to enjoy some warmth after the long, cold winter. The further north, the bigger the party!

The midsummer festival in Utne, Norway. In Norway, it is traditional to light fires on Midsummer Eve.

Karl's Midsummer's Eve

'Last night was Midsummer's Eve. My friend and I went around the village collecting fuel for the bonfire. In the evening, my older brother's friends cut down a fir tree. The girls decorated it with wreaths of leaves and red ribbons. It was set alight and the young men quickly collected the wreaths. The young men and women looked at each other through the wreaths to see who they might marry!'
Karl, Bohemia, Germany

The midsummer festival comes from ancient customs. Many ancient stone circles and **monuments**, such as Stonehenge, were built so that the sun would rise over them in a certain way on Midsummer's Day. The festival was later adopted by Christians; 23 June was named as St John the Baptist Day.

The celebrations revolve around fire and water. In Estonia and Finland, the parties last a whole week. Everyone dances and sings around a bonfire. In Poland, the girls wear **wreaths** of flowers on their heads. Then they take off their wreaths, place a lighted candle on them and let them float down the river.

Midsummer is celebrated in North Africa too. In Algeria and Morocco, people light bonfires. The bonfire smoke is supposed to have magical properties. It to said to cure the sick, get rid of bad luck, and even stop people's hair from falling out!

People dancing around the Stonehenge monument in England at Midsummer.

Days to Remember in the USA, June and July

Schoolchildren in the USA show loyalty to their flag every day at school.

National Flag Day

On 14 June, it is National Flag Day. Flag Day was first celebrated in 1877, one hundred years after the USA adopted its own national flag, the Stars and Stripes. But the day was not made a **national holiday** until 1949, when President Harry Truman introduced it. Ever since then, Americans have been encouraged to display the Stars and Stripes outside their homes and businesses on 14 June.

Independence Day

Each year, 4 July is celebrated as the day when the USA broke away from British rule, back in 1776. From that time onwards, the USA ran itself as an independent country. Americans celebrate in style, with parades, picnics and fireworks.

The parades begin in the morning. Across the USA, local baseball teams, school bands and **baton-twirlers** march through their town. People gather in the streets to watch, munching popcorn and waving little US flags.

Then it is time for a picnic or barbecue. Some families get together at home, but many people head outdoors, to the beach or to a lake. In the evening, there are fireworks displays in most US cities.

A spectacular fireworks display in New York, USA, to celebrate 4 July.

Carlos's 4th of July

'This 4th of July, I played my drum in the parade and then we were off to the beach for a barbecue. We filled up on burgers, potato salad and corn on the cob, and drank cola. In the evening we went to the fireworks display. Some fireworks were in the colours of our flag – red, white and blue. People here are very proud of their country.'

Carlos, California, USA

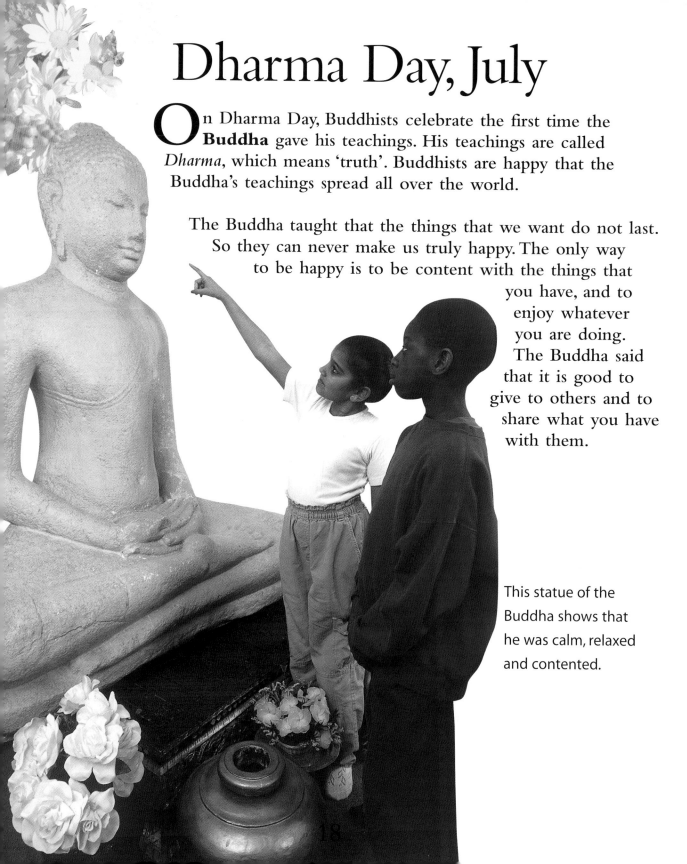

Dharma Day, July

On Dharma Day, Buddhists celebrate the first time the **Buddha** gave his teachings. His teachings are called *Dharma*, which means 'truth'. Buddhists are happy that the Buddha's teachings spread all over the world.

The Buddha taught that the things that we want do not last. So they can never make us truly happy. The only way to be happy is to be content with the things that you have, and to enjoy whatever you are doing. The Buddha said that it is good to give to others and to share what you have with them.

This statue of the Buddha shows that he was calm, relaxed and contented.

18

Sonia's Dharma Day

'On Dharma Day we heard about the Tibetan saint, Milarepa. His **Guru** tested his faith. He made him build, knock down and rebuild a platform loads of times. Milarepa got really fed up until he understood he was being tested. He realized that he should keep his faith even during difficult times. Then we talked about how we can learn from tricky situations. I enjoyed spending time with my Buddhist friends on Dharma Day.'
Sonia, Sydney, Australia

On Dharma Day, people go to the temple to listen to the Buddha's teachings from the holy book, the *Pali Canon*. Often a Buddhist teacher will read a story from the *Pali Canon* with the children and they discuss it. People take part in *puja* (worship) and they meditate. To meditate, they sit quietly and still with their thoughts. It helps them to become calm, happy and wise. People bring vegetarian food to share afterwards.

A young monk in Burma is studying the *Pali Canon*.

The Birth of Haile Selassie, 23 July

All over the world, Rastafarians celebrate the birth of Ras Tafari. Ras Tafari became Emperor of Ethiopia, Africa, in 1930. He took the name Emperor Haile Selassie.

Tracy's celebrations

'Last night we celebrated Haile Selassie's birthday. There were speeches about how important he is and people talked about our own heroes from Barbados. My dad joined in the drumming. I ate conkies, made from plantains (like bananas), sugar and cinnamon. To drink there was peanut punch, which contains peanut butter, milk, sugar and lime. Everyone was really friendly there and I loved dancing to the music.'

Tracy, Bridgetown, Barbados

Rastafarians on the Caribbean island of Jamaica joyfully waving the Rastafarian flag, which has the colours of the Ethiopian flag.

Rastafarians believe that Haile Selassie was a god in human form. They believe he was important because he stood up for black people. Black people suffered because long ago they were taken away from Africa as slaves and treated badly. Even today, many black people are treated unfairly. Rastafarians believe that black people will be saved by returning to their first home, Africa.

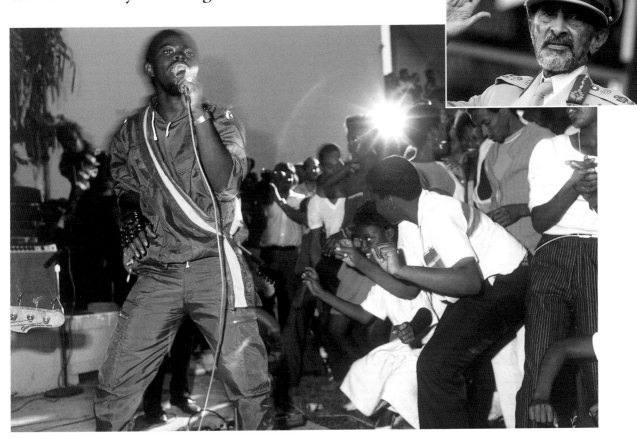

Above: Emperor Haile Selassie. Below: People in Jamaica dance to the sounds of reggae.

Today, Haile Selassie's birthday celebrations are biggest in the Caribbean islands, where the faith began. The climate is **tropical** and the weather is hot. Rastafarians come to gatherings and concerts. Many wear the colours of the Ethiopian flag – yellow, red, green and black. The atmosphere is relaxed. There is Rastafarian drumming and chanting, and people dance to **reggae**. Often there are exhibitions of African art, and delicious **vegetarian** food is shared out.

21

Raksha Bandhan, July or August

Here is the story behind this Hindu festival. Once, the wicked demon-king Bali fought a god called Indra. Bali drove Indra out. Indra's wife, Sachi, was deeply upset. She went to ask the god Vishnu for help. He gave her a bracelet, made from threads, to tie around Indra's wrist. Indra fought another battle with Bali. This time, Indra defeated the demon-king because of the luck and protection offered by the bracelet. He won back his kingdom.

Sisters in Nepal making offerings to their brother on the occasion of Raksha Bandhan.

Kunj's Raksha Bandhan

'Mum told me that *raksha* means "protection" and *bandhan* means "to tie". At this festival, all brothers and sisters – grown-ups too – show how much they love each other. I haven't got a sister so my cousin Nina gave me a *rakhi*. It's supposed to bring good luck and protection like in the story. In return, I gave Nina some money and she chose a pair of earrings.'

Kunj, Gujarat, India

Raksha Bandhan is a festival to help families to feel closer. In northern India, it also marks the start of the farming year.

First, the sister makes a mark on her brother's forehead with *kum-kum* paste, made from a red powder. She places some grains of rice on the mark. Next, she ties a *rakhi* (thread bracelet) around her brother's wrist and puts a sweet called *barfi* in his mouth. She says a little prayer for God to look after him. In return, the brother promises to protect his sister from harm, and he offers her a present.

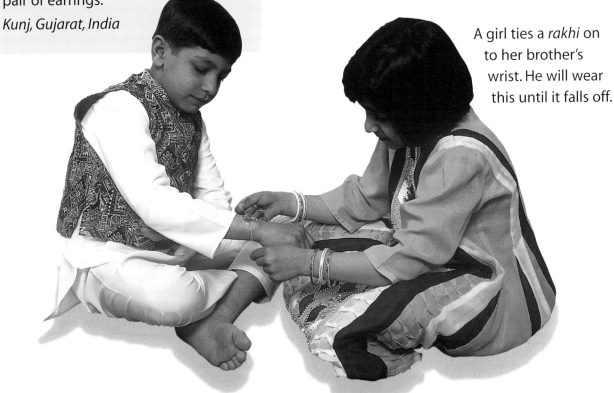

A girl ties a *rakhi* on to her brother's wrist. He will wear this until it falls off.

Krishna Janmashtami, August or September

At this joyful festival, Hindus celebrate Krishna's birth. Krishna is one of the forms of God and he is very special to many Hindus.

As it is an important festival, Hindus **fast** during the day. In the evening, people gather at the *mandir*, the Hindu temple. It is believed that Krishna was born at midnight, so they wait eagerly for the moment. Everybody sings *bhajans* (hymns) about Krishna and there is dancing too. As midnight approaches, there is an atmosphere of great excitement and joy.

Meera's Krishna Janmashtami

'On Krishna's birthday we went to the *mandir*. People were singing and playing Indian musical instruments. I played the *tabla* – a small drum. At midnight, all the kids took it in turn to rock Krishna's cradle and we offered dishes of sweets to him. He looked really cute! By this time, we were very hungry. We ate rice, **dhal** and vegetables, and later we got to eat Krishna's sweets too.'

Meera, Kampala, Uganda

Worshippers at the temple, each holding a little tray with a candle for the *arti* ceremony held at midnight.

An image of baby Krishna on display for his birthday in Singapore. He is being rocked like a real baby!

In the *mandir*, there is an image of baby Krishna in a cradle. At midnight, everyone gathers around the cradle for the *arti* ceremony. This involves moving lamps in circles in front of baby Krishna. People ring bells and blow a **conch shell** to announce the happy arrival.

In some places, fruit and sweets are shared out after midnight. In others, there's a proper Indian meal with rice and vegetables. Many Hindus eat tasty dishes made with milk and butter because it is said that Krishna loved dairy foods.

The *Guru Granth Sahib*, September

Sikhs gather at this festival to celebrate their holy book, the *Guru Granth Sahib*. It contains hymns called *shabads*, which were written by the Sikh **Gurus** – and also by Hindu and Muslim holy men. The *shabads* are written in a language called Gurmukhi, the written form of the Indian language, Punjabi. They are poems that can be sung to music. Music is extremely important in Sikh worship.

Both men and women may read from the *Guru Granth Sahib*.

In 1708, the tenth Guru, Guru Gobind Singh, announced that he was the last human Guru. From then on, Sikhs were to use the *Guru Granth Sahib* as their guide. They show great respect to their holy book, honouring it just like the human Gurus.

26

As Sikhs enter the *gurdwara*, they bow and pray to the Guru Granth Sahib. When it is not being read, it is covered and kept in a special place in the *gurdwara*.

At the festival, people come to the *gurdwara* to worship. They think about how best to follow the teachings of their holy book.

Young people learn Gurmukhi so they can read their holy book.

Kiran's celebrations

'Two days before the festival, my mum went to the *gurdwara* to help read our holy book. The reading of the whole book is called *Akhand Path* and it takes 48 hours! We do it at all the festivals. On the day, we sang hymns and listened to a talk about why our holy book is important. Afterwards we had our shared meal, called *langar*. I had two portions of *kheer* for dessert.'
Kiran, Mombasa, Kenya

Lailat ul-Miraj

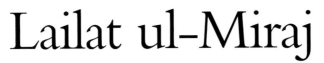

On this night, Muslims celebrate the **Prophet Muhammad's** ﷺ extraordinary journey through the heavens.

When the Prophet Muhammad ﷺ was about fifty, he was having a terrible time. It was ten years since he had received the message from **Allah** to go out and preach about the one true God. But few believed him. People laughed at him and he was treated badly.

It is said that one night the angel Jibril (Gabriel) shook Muhammad ﷺ awake and took him to Jerusalem on a winged animal called *al-Buraq* (the lightning). He was taken up through the seven heavens, where he met all the earlier Jewish prophets – also honoured by Muslims. He rose to Allah's presence, a place of great peace and pure light. Here it was decided that Muslims should pray five times a day.

It is said that Muhammad ﷺ rose to heaven from a rock that lies inside the stunning Dome of the Rock mosque in Jerusalem.

Hussein's Lailat ul-Miraj

'I think the Prophet ﷺ was ever so brave to keep his faith and preach about Allah even when hardly anyone would listen. At school, we talked about Muhammad's ﷺ night journey and tried to imagine the amazing winged animal. On Lailat ul-Miraj, they say that there is a special moment in the middle of the night when our prayers are granted. I stayed awake long after bedtime, waiting for that moment.'
Hussein, Al Khawr, Qatar

A father and son stay up late to pray on Lailat ul-Miraj.

The night journey to the heavens gave Muhammad ﷺ great strength at a difficult time in his life.

On Lailat ul-Miraj, some people stay up all night praying. Children practise saying their prayers and learn about the meaning of Muhammad's ﷺ night journey.

29

Calendar of festivals

Most religions follow a lunar calendar, based on the moon's movements, rather than a solar calendar. They adjust the calendar to keep the festivals in their season. Muslims don't adjust their calendar, so the festivals can be at any time of the year and are not related to the seasons. Sikh festivals are usually three days long because they include the two-day reading of the Sikh holy book before the festival day.

2004

Pentecost	30 May
Poson Day	9 June
Shavuot	13–14 June
Flag Day	14 June
The Martyrdom of Guru Arjan	16 June
Midsummer's Day	21 June
American Independence Day	4 July
Dharma Day	15 July
The Birth of Haile Selassie	23 July
Raksha Bandhan	30 August
The Guru Granth Sahib	1 September
Krishna Janmashtami	6 September
Lailat ul-Miraj	12 September

2005

Pentecost	15 May
Poson Day	9 June
Shavuot	13–14 June
Flag Day	14 June
The Martyrdom of Guru Arjan	16 June
Midsummer's Day	21 June
American Independence Day	4 July
Dharma Day	15 July
The Birth of Haile Selassie	23 July
Raksha Bandhan	19 August
Krishna Janmashtami	27 August
The Guru Granth Sahib	1 September
Lailat ul-Miraj	1 September

2006

Shavuot	2–3 June
Pentecost	4 June
Poson Day	9 June
Flag Day	14 June
The Martyrdom of Guru Arjan	16 June
Midsummer's Day	21 June
American Independence Day	4 July
Dharma Day	15 July
The Birth of Haile Selassie	23 July
Raksha Bandhan	9 August
Krishna Janmashtami	16 August
Lailat ul-Miraj	22 August
The Guru Granth Sahib	1 September

Glossary

Allah The Muslim name for God.

baptism A Christian ceremony. Water is poured on to a person to welcome him or her to the Church.

baton-twirlers People who march with a band, holding a long stick that they throw in the air in a special way.

Buddha The man who started the Buddhist religion.

conch shell The outer shell of a sea creature called a conch.

dhal A dish made with lentils or other pulses.

fast To go without food or without certain foods. Some Hindus even go without water on the day of Krishna Janmashtami.

first fruits The first produce of the season, often offered to God.

gurdwara The building where Sikhs go to meet and worship.

Guru A holy Buddhist or Sikh teacher.

kheer An Indian dessert made with rice, milk and sugar.

monuments Ancient buildings that were made to celebrate something, such as the sun at midsummer.

national holiday An important day that is a holiday in the whole country.

northern hemisphere The northern half of the Earth. The southern half of the Earth is called the southern hemisphere.

offerings Food, flowers or other gifts that are placed in front of statues of the Buddha to give thanks for his teachings.

Prophet Muhammad ﷺ Muslims believe that Muhammad ﷺ was the last prophet to bring Allah's message to the world.

reggae A kind of popular music with a strong beat.

synagogue The building where Jewish people meet and worship.

Ten Commandments The most important rules for Jewish people about how to live and worship. It is believed that they were given by God to the Jewish people.

tropical Countries that are tropical are in the tropics, the hottest area of the world. This area is just above and just below the Equator, an imaginary line drawn around the middle of the Earth.

vegetarian A type of food that contains no meat or fish, or a person who does not eat meat or fish.

wreath A circle of flowers or leaves.

Further Information

Books for Children

Celebrate Buddhist Festivals by Clive and Jane Erricker (Heinemann Library, 1996)

Celebrate Christian Festivals by Jan Thompson (Heinemann Library, 1996)

Celebrate Hindu Festivals by Dilip Kadodwala, Paul Gateshill (Heinemann Library, 1996)

Celebrate Islamic Festivals by Khadijah Knight (Heinemann Library, 1996)

Celebrate Jewish Festivals by Angela Wood (Heinemann Library, 1996)

Celebrate Sikh Festivals by John Coutts (Heinemann Library, 1996)

My Buddhist Year, My Christian Year, My Hindu Year, My Jewish Year, My Muslim Year, My Sikh Year, all by Cath Senker (Hodder Wayland, 2002-2003)

Websites

www.theresite.org.uk/
website.lineone.net/~jlancs/startpage.htm

Index

All numbers in **bold** refer to pictures as well as text.